RAILS AROUND MANCHESTER

MIKE RHODES

AMBERLEY

First published 2025

Amberley Publishing
The Hill, Stroud
Gloucestershire, GL5 4EP

www.amberley-books.com

ISBN 978 1 3981 2103 4 (print)
ISBN 978 1 3981 2104 1 (ebook)

British Library Cataloguing in Publication Data.
A catalogue record for this book is available from the British Library.

Origination by Amberley Publishing.
Printed in the UK.

Appointed GPSR EU Representative: Easy Access System Europe Oü, 16879218
Address: Mustamäe tee 50, 10621, Tallinn, Estonia
Contact Details: gpsr.requests@easproject.com, +358 40 500 3575

Abbreviations

BMU Battery Multiple Unit; BR British Railways; BRCW Birmingham Railway Carriage & Wagon; BREL British Rail Engineering Limited; CEGB Central Electricity Generating Board; CEMEX Cementos Mexicanos; CLC Cheshire Lines Committee; DMU Diesel Multiple Unit; DVT Driving Van Trailer; ECS Empty Coaching Stock, ELR East Lancashire Railway; ELRly East Lancs Railway; EMD Electro Motive Diesel; EMU Electric Multiple Unit; EWS English Welsh & Scottish; FLHH Freight Liner Heavy Haul; FLT Freight Liner Terminal; GBRF GB Railfreight; GCR Great Central Railway; GE General Electric; GEML Great Eastern Main Line; GMCA Greater Manchester Combined Authority; GMCC Greater Manchester County Council; GMEX Greater Manchester Exhibition Centre; GMPTE Greater Manchester Passenger Transport Executive; GMT Greater Manchester Transport; GNR Great Northern Railway; HMP Her Majesty's Prison; HST High Speed Train; ICI Imperial Chemical Industries; L&MR Liverpool & Manchester Railway; LMS London Midland & Scottish; LNER London North Eastern Railway; LNWR London North Western Railway; M&BR Manchester & Birmingham Railway; M&SR Manchester & Sheffield Railway; MB&BR Manchester Bolton & Bury Railway; MSJ&AR Manchester South Junction & Altrincham Railway; NCB National Coal Board; NRM National Railway Museum; NSE Network South East; RC&WCo Railway Carriage & Wagon Company; RES Rail Express Systems; RSH Robert Stephenson & Hawthorn; SA&MR Sheffield Ashton & Manchester Railway; SNCF Société Nationale des Chermins de fer Français; SuO Sundays Only; TMD Traction Motive Power Depot; TPE Trans Pennine Express; UK United Kingdom; VT Virgin Trains; WCML West Coast Main Line; WR Western Region.

Introduction

For the purpose of this book the extent of the railways covered around Manchester are based on the area of validity of the Manchester Wayfarer Ticket. The extremities on the lines radiating out from the city are thus: Parbold/Wigan, Chorley, Bolton, Bury, Rochdale, Littleborough, Oldham, Mossley, Hadfield, Edale, Buxton, Macclesfield, Holmes Chapel, Manchester Airport, Altrincham/Northwich and Warrington.

The author's first adventure to Manchester took place way back in August 1963 and subsequent excursions followed throughout the 1960s when visits were made to the various motive power depots during the closing years of the steam era. Regular visits have continued over the years to the present day to record the ever-changing railway scene.

Manchester's railway journey began on 19 September 1830 when the Liverpool & Manchester Railway opened a line which terminated at a purpose-built station in Liverpool Road on the edge of the city centre. In 1838 the Manchester, Bolton & Bury Railway constructed a line out to Bolton. This was followed in July 1839 by the arrival of the Manchester & Leeds Railway, which terminated at a station adjacent to Oldham Road, again on the periphery of the city centre. Liverpool Road and Oldham Road stations were both closed in 1844 following the grand opening of the L&Y's new Victoria station on 1 January. Both buildings remained in use as goods depots for many more years and the former eventually became a science museum building.

Meanwhile to the south the Manchester & Birmingham Railway eventually reached the city, after constructing the imposing Stockport Viaduct, when it opened a new station at Store Street in May 1842. This original simple two-platform affair later mushroomed into what became known as first London Road and then, from 1960, Piccadilly. Close on its heels was the Sheffield, Ashton & Manchester Railway, which shared tracks with the M&BR from Ardwick to Store Street. The railway system around Manchester greatly expanded over the next forty years with new lines opened by the CLC, L&Y, LNWR and the Midland, with the former being responsible for the line out of Manchester Central towards Didsbury and beyond to New Mills in July 1880. Just a few years later, on 30 June 1884, the LNWR opened Manchester Exchange station, which catered for services to Hull, Leeds, Liverpool, Newcastle and North Wales.

Of some significance was the construction of the line to Altrincham, which was instigated by the Manchester South Junction & Altrincham Railway in 1849, the Midland Railway's incursion towards Buxton in 1863 and construction of the line from New Mills to Sheffield by the same company in 1894, which included boring out the Dore & Totley Tunnel. The last significant addition to the railway network was the Stockport by-pass line between Longsight and Wilmslow, which was opened by the LNWR In 1909.

In 2023 the extended Manchester rail network (as defined by the Wayfarer Ticket boundary) comprised 162 route miles and served 130 stations. The oldest stations that had been in continuous use were Eccles, Earlestown and Patricroft, which were situated on the original 1830-built main line from Liverpool. Since 1977 British Railways/Network Rail had opened fifteen new stations, the most recent being Horwich Parkway in 1999. Since the 1990s the development of Metrolink had taken preference over the opening of any more new railway stations. Over the years more than 140 stations had disappeared from the city's railway map, with the most recent (other than Metrolink conversions) being Miles Platting in May 1995.

Prominent station closures over the years have included Bacup (1966), Bolton Great Moor Street (1954), Bury Knowsley Street (1970), Bury Bolton Street (1991), Macclesfield Hibel Road (1960), Manchester Central (1969), Manchester Exchange (1969), Manchester Liverpool Road (1844), Manchester Mayfield (1960), Manchester Oldham Road (1844), Oldham Central (1966), Oldham Mumps (2009), Old Trafford Halt (2017), Ramsbottom/Rawtenstall (1972) and Stockport Tiviot Dale (1967). Two stations which have delightful names are Bess o' th' Barn and Irlams o' th' Height. Whilst the former is now a Metrolink station the latter was closed in 1956.

The principal MPDs which provided the locomotives for trains serving Manchester London Road (Piccadilly) were Longsight (9A) and Stockport Edgeley (9B). The former was closed to steam in 1965 and developed over the years as a modern TMD, which successively serviced the various forms of modern diesel and electric traction through to the present day. Stockport Edgeley shed was closed in May 1968. The last pockets of Jubilees and Britannias in the Manchester area were allocated to Edgeley with Nos 45596 *Bahamas**, 45632 *Tonga*, 70004 *William Shakespeare**, 70015 *Apollo* and 70021 *Morning Star** being noted on visits in August 1965 and December 1966*. Standard Class 2 Tanks Nos 84013/4/7 were also present on the earlier visit having been transferred in from Bolton. Stockport also had a freight shed on the former CLC line at Heaton Mersey. Here some of the last of Stanier's 2-6-0 Crab engines could be found with seven of the type present on 7 August 1965. They were rubbing shoulders with five LMS Class 4MT 2-6-0s of the No. 43xxx series.

Somewhat of an enigma was Gorton shed, which had been built by the Great Central Railway and also provided engines for trains out of London Road. However, having been coded 39A, the depot assumed the code of 9G in 1959 and finally divested itself of the last classes of Eastern Region steam three years later.

To the west of the city centre large steam sheds had been established by the CLC/MR at Trafford Park (9E) and by the LNWR at Patricroft (9H). The latter was known for its large allocation of Standard Class 5MT 4-6-0s with no less than thirty-two of the type present on shed on 11 December 1966, including class leader No. 73000. There were also five Standard Class 3 2-6-2 tank engines in attendance. The Bolton line also possessed engine sheds at Agecroft (9J) and Bolton (9K). None of these depots had any facilities to service diesel locomotives and all four were closed with the elimination of steam between 1966 and 1968.

To the east of Manchester Victoria lay the former L&Y engine shed at Newton Heath (9D). This was the last depot with an allocation of steam locomotives, with the last fires being dropped on 1 July 1968. The shed was also developed as a maintenance centre for diesel multiple units and has been responsible for a wide range of class types of both first and second generation diesel unit types. It was still functioning as such in 2025.

To complete the round up of depots in the region MPDs were also located at Macclesfield (9C), Reddish (also 9C), Buxton (9L), Bury (9M) and Oldham Lees (9P). Buxton shed serviced some of the locos employed on the Peak Forest stone trains particularly over the transition from steam to diesel in the mid-1960s; it also had a small allocation of LNER-designed J94 0-6-0 saddle tanks, which were used on the Cromford & High Peak Railway (closed on 2 October 1967), with Nos 68012/68/79 being present on 7 August 1965 along with a small number of withdrawn Midland 4Fs. Reddish depot was primarily the base for the Woodhead electrics and Hadfield multiple units, although other unusual types could sometimes be found there such as four Shenfield electric sets on 27 August 1966.

Whilst Buckley Wells at Bury was home to the third rail electric units the abandoned steam shed was later used to store main line electric locos, with twenty-two of types AL2/3/4 and five EM2s being recorded on shed on 24 July 1969. Locomotive building/repair works in the region had been situated at Gorton (1848–1964) and Horwich (1886–1983). A new TMD was built at Ardwick and opened in 2006 to service and maintain the Class 185 diesel units; the depot was later adapted to additionally service Class 350/4 electric units.

The Manchester to Bury line via Crumpsall had opened in 1879. The L&Y Railway was a very progressive company and electrified the line in 1916 using a 1200v dc side collection system. The rolling stock consisted of thirty-eight motor cars and twenty-eight trailers and could operate in a variety of formations of between two and five cars. These units were replaced in 1959 by twenty-six two-car sets, which were built at BR's Wolverton Works and were classified as Class 504. In their early years they operated in pairs. However, there was always too many sets for the service and eight sets had been laid up by the early 1970s with several cars eventually being scrapped during the following decade. Most of the others continued to see some use until closure of the system on 17 August 1991 when work began on the first line of the new Metrolink network.

The next electrification scheme was undertaken by the LMS in 1931 when the original MSJ&A Railway line between Manchester London Road and Altrincham was electrified using the 1500v dc overhead system. The coaching stock comprised twenty-two three-car sets, which were built at Metro-Cammell in Birmingham. If they had survived long enough they would have been designated Class 505. The operation was cut back to Oxford Road in 1961 and they continued in service until 1971 when the line was converted to operation using 25kv ac. The ubiquitous Class 304 units then assumed responsibility for the service.

It had been proposed before the Second World War to electrify the line from Sheffield to Manchester over the Woodhead Pass. However, the hostilities greatly delayed this adventurous scheme. Nevertheless on 22 September 1954 such a service was inaugurated again using the 1500v dc system. A stopping service was introduced over the Guide Bridge route as far as Hadfield using a fleet of eight three-car electric sets, which were built by BRCW; they were designated as Class 506. These continued in service until December 1984 when the remnants of the line were converted to 25kv ac pick-up and Classes 303/04/05 units were deployed.

The Woodhead line was devised as an important freight route connecting South Yorkshire with Manchester and beyond. A large marshalling yard was laid out at Mottram and it became an important route for the transhipment of coal, particularly to Fiddlers Ferry Power Station. A prototype electric locomotive was built at Doncaster in 1941 and was eventually numbered (E)26000, later acquiring the name *Tommy*. The production series comprised Nos (E)26001–57 and were built at Gorton between 1950 and 1953 and were designated as Type EM1 (76); these were principally used on freight services. Seven additional locos, allocated Nos (E)27000–6, were designated as Type EM2 (77) and were for use on passenger trains. A basic hourly schedule was provided between Manchester and Sheffield. The passenger service was withdrawn on 5 January 1970 and the Woodhead route was completely closed beyond Hadfield on 18 July 1981. Six of the EM2s were sold to the Dutch Railways for further use.

The electrification of the WCML was a long drawn-out affair. The lines from Crewe to Manchester via Stockport and Macclesfield were the first sections to be energised in 1959/60; the Styal line was also treated at the same time. The Class AM4 (304) electric units were introduced specifically for the local services in the north-west. At the same time the first mainline locos, Class AL1 (81), were being built at BRCW for loco-hauled trains. The first of these two types were allocated to Longsight depot for maintenance purposes. Full electrification between

Manchester and London Euston was not achieved until April 1966, by which time there were around 200 electric locos available for service.

There have been four significant improvement schemes over the last forty years, which have helped to redefine the pattern of services across the city. On 29 April 1986 a new connecting chord was opened to the east of Hazel Grove, which then allowed trains to Sheffield to be routed via Stockport. Of great significance was the opening of the Windsor Link at Salford in May 1988, which enabled services from north Lancashire to be routed via Oxford Road and Piccadilly and linked to services on the south-east side.

To coincide with the opening of a second terminal at Manchester Airport an entirely new station was built, which opened up further travelling opportunities. Initially only two platforms were provided but a further two have since been added and it is directly connected to the Metrolink network. Finally the Ordsall Chord was opened on 10 December 2017 enabling trains to travel directly between Piccadilly and Victoria stations for the first time.

Manchester has benefitted from a number of prestigiously named trains over the years. One of the earliest was the 'Palatine', which ran between Manchester Central and London St Pancras between the years 1938–64. Other long-standing trains were the 'Mancunian' (1927–66) between London Road (Piccadilly) and London Euston; the 'Pines Express' (1927–67) 1095, which may have departed Piccadilly for Bournemouth West and other south coast destinations behind a 'Semi' in the 1950s; and the Harwich Boat Train (1963–88). which ran under headcode 1E87 and was usually hauled by a well-turned-out Stratford-based Class 37. The Pines was revived for a short period at the end of the 1990s with HSTs being the designated motive power.

The 'Midland Pullman' (1960–66) ran between Manchester Central and London St Pancras, departing Central at 08.50 and St Pancras at 18.10. The train was made up of one of the two stylish Blue Pullman sets, which were maintained at Reddish. Meanwhile over at Victoria the 'Belfast Boat Express' (1960–75) 1P42 provided a service to Heysham to connect with the Irish Sea ferry crossing. It was steam-hauled for the last time on 4 May 1968 by Carnforth's Black 5 No. 45342, which departed on time at 21.00.

Whilst steam could still be seen at Victoria and Exchange stations right to the end, Piccadilly only reverberated to the sound of diesel traction (and the silence of electrics) from the early 1960s onwards. Due to the constraints of the through lines at Piccadilly most freight services were routed through Victoria. For many years newspaper traffic was an important aspect of the local railway scene and Red Bank Sidings were a well-known location on the railway map.

The Manchester tram network is the largest in the UK and serves ninety-nine stops over a system which comprises 62 route miles. The first line was opened between Bury Interchange and Piccadilly station on 6 April 1992. Most of the route had previously been part of the railway network. The second line to Altrincham opened on 15 June 1992. Other sections which were built on former railway formations included the line from Oldham to Rochdale and Old Trafford to East Didsbury. The last line to open was that to the Trafford Centre on 22 March 2020. The system is operated by 147 Bombardier-built M5000 single-articulated trams. The last of the original thirty-two Italian-built T68/A trams were withdrawn in 2014.

With regards to the myth that it always rains in Manchester – the reader can judge for themselves from this comprehensive selection of the author's photographs.

When Manchester Victoria was opened on 1 January 1844 it was a modest two-platform affair. By 1904 it had reached its maximum size of seventeen platforms. Built to replace both Oldham Road and Liverpool Road, it had ten bay platforms on the south side, which were built on what had previously been a burial ground (bodies were exhumed during reconstruction works in 2013–15 and interred at the Southern Cemetery in Chorlton). Local services to Bury, Huddersfield, Oldham, Rochdale and Stalybridge generally departed from these bays. *Above:* Bury electric unit Nos 77170 and 65449 in blue and grey is seen departing Victoria with a train for Bury on 9 June 1984. These trains tended to use platforms 4 and 5, with 1 to 3 having fallen out of use. *Below:* Newton Heath's Class 104 set Nos 53527 and 53435 is seen waiting to depart platform 8 with a Rochdale bound train on the same date. Just visible is one of the single-car Class 128 Gloucester RC&W Co. parcels units.

Newspaper trains had long been a feature of Victoria/Exchange stations as Manchester was the UK's second city with regards to printing of the daily tabloids. On 27 July 1985 Class 25 No. 25259 (D7609) waits to depart platform 9 with two vans. For many years Red Bank Sidings had been used to stable rakes of these vans during the day but they were abandoned in 1990. The Type 2 was built at Derby in April 1966.

Peaks or Class 45s and 46s were a common sight at all four of Manchester's principal stations. No. 45144 (D55) *Royal Signals* was photographed approaching Victoria from the east on 3 July 1984 with the 14.20 Newcastle Central to Liverpool Lime Street. Number 45144 was turned out from Crewe Works in September 1962 and remained in service until December 1987; it was scrapped the following year.

With InterCity branding on the coaches Peak Class 45 No. 45134 waits to depart platform 12 on 19 June 1985 with the 16.05 Liverpool Lime Street to Newcastle Central. Platforms 12 to 17 were built on land which was previously occupied by the New Bridge Street Workhouse. The station roof was badly damaged by enemy bombing in December 1940 and never properly reinstated. This part of the station reverted back to development with the construction of the O2 Arena (now known as the AO Arena) in 1992–94. A Class 108 diesel unit idles away on one of the through roads.

Back in the 1920s/30s the LMS inaugurated a number of trains centred on Manchester under the banner of 'Club Trains'. These were resurrected by Regional Railways in the early 1990s. Class 37 No. 37419 (D6991) was photographed at platform 16 on 16 July 1991 with the 17.14 departure to Blackpool North. The station clock on platform 12, above the parcel's subway entrance, is showing 16.45.

A Class 56 and a Class 142 Pacer neatly frame the refreshment rooms on platform 12. Here a cheese sandwich and a fruit pie could be purchased for a modest fee. Nowadays station fayre consists of expensive fancy-named coffees and baguette-type rolls or the like. Oh for the old Manchester Victoria – it may have been decrepit but it certainly had character.

There were three through lines between platforms 11 and 12, one of which was used for stabling locos on. Back in the day these would have been banking engines to assist trains up the Miles Platting Bank. On 22 October 1991 Class 60 No. 60058 *John Howard* and Class 47s Nos 47357 (D1876) and 47355 (D1836) were caught at rest whilst three railway workers attend to the points' mechanism.

On 9 September 1992 Type 5 Class 60 No. 60021 *Pen-y-Ghent* is seen accelerating towards Miles Platting bank with 6E31 consisting of a rake of empty 100-ton bogie tankers travelling from the Weaste Tar Distiller depot to Port Clarence on Teesside. The name '*Penyghent*' was previously carried by Class 44 Peak No. D8, which is now preserved and was one of the first ten of the Sulzer Type 4s, which were all named after mountains.

Platform 11 was connected through to the erstwhile Manchester Exchange platform 3 and the combined platform was claimed to be the longest in Europe at 2,238 feet. Cross-overs to the adjacent track enabled more than one train to use the platform at the same time. *Above:* On 9 September 1992 Class 158 No. 158902 waits to depart with a train from York to Liverpool Lime Street. This was one of ten such units which were originally painted in West Yorkshire Metro red and white. Class 31 No. 31407 (D5640) is idling on the stabling road. *Below:* A meagre looking train has been provided for the long journey to Llandudno in the form of two-car Sprinter Class 150 No. 150249 on 22 October 1991. Class 37 No. 37426 (D6999) can be glimpsed behind the steel stanchions.

Seen passing through the middle on 8 May 1985 with a short train of low-sided wagons containing concrete sleepers is Class 47 No. 47207 (D1857), complete with 'West Highland Terrier' emblem on the side (indicating it was once allocated to Glasgow's Eastfield TMD). This train may have been bound for the engineering yard at Castleton. Number 47207 was built at Crewe in August 1965 and withdrawn on 10 September 2004.

Class 104 diesel unit Nos. 53436 and 53488 are seen against an industrial background as they approach Victoria with a local train on 25 March 1985. This view is looking across to HMP Strangeways (on the left), which was opened in 1869 and administered the death penalty sentence until 1964. The thin brick chimney on the right was part of the Strangeways Brewery complex. The skyline now looks somewhat different.

There were eight tracks on the immediate approach to Victoria from the west, including the track which served platform 5 at Exchange station (seen still in situ on the left). Class 47 No. 47434 (D1549) has just passed Deal Street Signal Box (closed on 31 July 1998) on its approach to Victoria with the 07.05 Liverpool Lime Street to Scarborough on 1 June 1985. The tall building above the rear of the train is the Grade II listed Threlfalls Brewery, which opened in 1896 and is now part of a business village complex.

Although Manchester Exchange station was closed on 5 May 1969, the footprint of the platforms remained untouched for many more years. Opened by the LNWR on 30 June 1884, it had two bay and three through platforms. Peak No. 45104 (D59) *The Royal Warwickshire Fusilier* is seen passing through what had been platform 3 on 5 January 1985 with the 07.50 Scarborough to Liverpool Lime Street. The splendid 1900s station façade is clearly visible above the rear of the train.

By 1994 the west approach to the station had been radically altered. Only four tracks can be seen in this view recorded on 9 July, which depicts Merseyrail-liveried Class 142 No. 142056 departing with an unidentified local train. Although the tracks through platforms 3 and 4 at Exchange have now been lifted the footbridge is still there. The site was eventually redeveloped with high-rise buildings in the twenty-first century. Victoria West Junction Signal Box was closed on 8 August 1993 and presents a somewhat forlorn sight.

The north side of the station was substantially rebuilt in 1992–94 with platforms 11 to 17 swept away. The new arrangement provided for four through platforms whilst part of the previous station area was occupied by the newly constructed O2 concert arena. Local trains are seen at the new platforms 5 and 6 in the form of Pacer No. 142012 and Sprinter No. 150207 on 21 June 1997.

Platforms 4 and 5 had latterly been used by the Bury electrics but were removed and replaced by the through Metrolink lines in 1992. The station was substantially rebuilt and reconfigured and now only has six platforms, two of which are the former bay platforms 9 and 10, which were renumbered to 1 and 2. The Class 144 diesel units were a joint enterprise between BREL and Walter Alexander's and were built in 1986/7. Number 144022 is seen at platform 2 (10) on 9 April 2009 with a Leeds bound train.

Preserved Class 50s Nos 50033 *Glorious* (D433) and 50007 *Hercules* (D407) can be seen on the Castlefield Arches having just passed under the former CLC Lines' wrought-iron girder bridge. This section of line was laid by the MSJ&AR in 1849 to connect with the LNWR's line out of Salford, seen in the foreground. The train was Pathfinder Tours' 'The Merseyman' 1Z44 06.35 Bristol Temple Meads to Liverpool Seaforth Docks via Worcester, Birmingham, Derby, Stockport and Manchester, which ran on 30 October 1993.

A view taken from Oldfield Road at Ordsall (Salford) on 4 July 1993 depicting Class 47 No. 47705 (D1957) in the erstwhile NSE colours with an unidentified 'Pullman' Excursion train. In the distance is the renovated and repurposed Manchester Central station building, which was opened by the CLC on 1 July 1880 and closed by BR on 5 May 1969. Visible on the left is the Granada Studio's 'Baker Street' Set and the late nineteenth-century GNR Co. Goods Warehouse building, which is located in Deansgate.

This is the former site of Ordsall Lane station, which was opened by the LNWR on 1 August 1849 and closed by BR on 4 February 1957. It had five through platforms and one bay with a number of adjacent sidings. Clearly visible over the trees is the long-closed series of wrought-iron truss-girder bridges, which were built in 1892 by the CLC to improve the access into Central station. The ICI Tunstead to Northwich limestone trains were normally routed via the Northenden line to the south of the city but on this occasion the train had been diverted through central Manchester due to Sunday engineering works. Class 37s Nos 37405 *Strathclyde Region* (D6982) and 37381 (D6984) were in charge of a westbound loaded rake of 1936-built hoppers on 20 June 1993. This section of line has since been electrified.

The Windsor Link at Salford was completed in May 1988 and revolutionised local services from the following year. The link is 765 yards long and connects the original 1830 L&MR/LNWR line to the 1838 MB&B/LYR line out of Salford and Manchester. It had only taken 150 years to connect the two. Sprinter unit No. 150135 has just left Salford Crescent station on 25 May 1992 with the 10.35 Southport to Buxton train via Bolton. The 150/1 units were originally built as two-car sets but some were increased to three-car formations with additional cars from disbanded 150/2 units.

Seen from the same vantage point of the Crescent Class 26s Nos 26040 (D5340) and 26001 (D5301) were photographed with 2C45, the 08.52 Manchester Victoria to Barrow working on 25 April 1992. This was one of a series of extra trains organised by Pathfinder Tours with unusual motive power in the north-west over the weekend of 25/26th. The Type 2s would have been more at home hauling coal trains in Scotland. To the right, many years ago, used to stand a wagon repair shed and a cattle station.

Salford Crescent was opened on 11 May 1987 and effectively replaced Pendleton (Broad Street) station, which was closed a few years later. Class 37 No. 37430 *Cwmbran* is drawing into platform 2 with the 07.16 Southport to Manchester Victoria 'Club Train' on 1 August 1991. The imposing building on the right was built as the Salford Electricity Generating Station, which opened in 1900. It supplied the power for the city's street lights and electric tramway system. Owned by the CEGB in 2023, it had been converted into office space.

Back in the mid-twentieth century Agecroft/Pendleton was home to a number of significant goods yards along with Agecroft MPD. The latter was opened by the LYR in 1889 and closed in October 1966. It only ever had an allocation of steam locos, which were predominantly 8Fs. On 13 March 1993 Class 26s Nos 26003 (D5303) and 26005 (D5305) were recorded in charge of Victoria Travel's 'The Cumbrian Tynesider' Carlisle Circular excursion, which ran via Sunderland, York, Wakefield and Manchester and is seen passing the shed site. Tarmac's asphalt plant is in the background.

Another of the 'Lancastrian Mini Excursions' was photographed at Agecroft on 25 April 1992 with Class 58 No. 58009 hauling 1T36 the 11.40 Southport to Manchester Victoria. Agecroft Power Station was commissioned in September 1925 and closed down in March 1993. It was supplied by coal from the adjacent colliery. There were three 0-4-0 Tank Engines built by RSH in 1948 to shunt the coal wagons. These were rendered redundant following the commissioning of a transporter bridge system. The track bed of the former line from the shed complex can be seen on the left.

Seen at the same location on 30 August 1993 is a pair of Class 104 DMUs with set No. 101680 leading comprising cars Nos 53204 and 53163. The train is probably a Blackpool North to Buxton working. Having recently closed, the power station cooling towers were demolished in May 1994. Having recently been transferred north from Laira to Longsight this unit was last noted in service in December 2003.

Just a few miles further along the line towards Bolton was located Kearsley Power Station. The Exchange Sidings were on the opposite side of the line to the power station and connected by a line which passed under the main line. The station was commissioned in 1929 and closed in 1982. Built by Robert Stevenson & Hawthorn, there were four of these electric locos operated by the CEGB, which dated from 1928 to 1946. It is believed No. 4, which was photographed on 18 July 1970, was the oldest.

In 1985 Bolton station was still controlled by semaphore signals, although not for much longer. Class 104 DMU Nos 53527 and 53475 is seen arriving on 1 June 1985 with the 17.00 Manchester Victoria to Blackburn. Bolton East Junction Signal Box was closed on 8 December 1985. The box also at one time controlled the line which branched off to the left towards Bury and Rochdale, until closure of the line on 5 October 1970.

Bolton Trinity Street station was opened in May 1838 by the Manchester, Bolton & Bury Railway. The line onwards to Preston was opened in 1841. The buildings in the background were swept away in 1987 to facilitate a new transport interchange, although the clock tower did survive; further major alterations were made in 2005–06 and a new bus/rail interchange was opened on 3 September 2017. Class 120 Swindon unit Nos 51576, 59582 and 51590 is seen departing with the 15.55 Blackpool North to Manchester Victoria on 1 June 1985.

A parcels bay was created on the west side of the station where at one time there had been a through platform. On 16 September 1991 Class 47 No. 47439 (D1555) was preparing to depart with 1V05, the 18.31 to Cardiff General. The through platform was later reinstated as platform 5 and was commissioned in September 2017.

This location has changed dramatically over the years. The lines diverge to pass either side of the platforms of what was Irlams 'o' th 'Height station, which was closed on 5 March 1956. There also used to be two more tracks on a separate embankment in front of the photographer. The headshunt of a carriage shed also existed in front of the train and in the immediate distance was Agecroft MPD. Seen amongst the desolation of what used to be is recently outshopped Class 37 No. 37422 (D6966) with the 17.30 Manchester Victoria to Southport 'Club Train' on 12 May 1993. The Agecroft Tarmac Plant is visible in the distance.

At one time Walkden had both a Low Level and a High Level station. The former was closed in March 1954. It was also the location of the 'Walkden Yard', which serviced engines for the Bridgewater Collieries Railway (NCB system from 1946) – a series of lines which connected a number of pits. Steam was still active on the system in 1970 but was rapidly being replaced by diesels. On 18 July Giesel Ejector-fitted Hunslet 0-6-0 Saddle Tank Works No. 3302 '*Stanley*', which was built in 1945, was photographed coming on to shed. *Stanley* saw further service at the Haig Colliery in Cumbria from 1971 to 1975, whilst the Walkden system was closed in 1986.

Ince station at Wigan always had a basic layout with minimal buildings. On a snowy 9 February 1991 Pacer unit No. 142052 has called with the 11.15 Wigan Wallgate to Stockport local stopping train. A short distance further along the route the line used to cross over a minor line which led from Springs Branch Junction to the Central Wagon Works. Here a number of steam locos were cut up in the early 1960s including Coronation Class Pacific No. 46243 *City of Lancaster*, which was noted at the works in March 1965. The line through Ince was electrified in 2024.

With HST power car No. 43123 leading and No. 43068 trailing the diverted 08.15 Glasgow Central to Poole Cross Country service is seen between Lostock and Bolton on 9 November 1991. On the extreme left is Middle Brook. The line between Bolton and Preston was electrified in 2018.

Further west, between Lostock and Horwich, a pair of Class 31s with No. 31306 (D5839) leading, are seen approaching Lostock Lane with a Manchester-bound spoil train on 22 June 1993. This view has now changed somewhat with the site huts and other engineering equipment having gone and a sea of electrification masts now disappearing into the distance.

Diversions away from the WCML were a common occurrence at weekends in the early 1990s. Class 47 No. 47550 (D1731) *University of Dundee* with a DVT behind was photographed passing Blackrod Junction Signal Box on 8 December 1991 with the 10.00 Blackpool North to London Euston. The box was opened by the LYR in 1881 and controlled the junction with the line to Horwich; it closed on 10 February 2013.

The Manchester to Bury line was built by the L&Y in 1879 and first electrified with a third rail in 1916. The original electric units were replaced in 1959 by twenty-six two-car sets, which were built at BR Wolverton. Although some were withdrawn early on, the remainder kept the service going until 1991 when the line was converted to a Metrolink service. Class 504 Nos 65445 and 77166 are seen at Bowker Vale with the 13.00 Manchester Victoria to Bury Interchange on 29 March 1991.

The original service had terminated at Bury Bolton Street station but this was closed in March 1980 when a new bus/rail interchange was opened. The rail line closed on 17 August 1991 and reopened as a Metro line on 6 April 1992. Class 504 set Nos 77177 and 65456 is seen crossing Radcliffe Viaduct with the 14.07 Bury Interchange to Manchester Victoria on 29 March 1991. Radcliffe station is in the background. All but two of the remaining sets were scrapped at MC Metals in Glasgow.

Following cessation of the electric service two sets were retained for possible preservation but only one was saved. Seen at Buckley Wells in Bury on 6 February 1994 are sets Nos 77182 and 65461 (since scrapped) and 77172 and 65451. The latterly used sets had been painted in the GMPTE colours.

At one time Bury had a comprehensive railway system with lines radiating out from both Bolton Street and Knowsley Street stations to Accrington, Bacup, Bolton, Castleton/Rochdale, Holcombe Brook, Manchester and Pendleton (Salford). Fortunately Bolton Street station was acquired by the East Lancashire Railway, which started running trains in July 1987. A wide variety of both steam and diesel locomotives have been operated over its thirty-six-year existence. This diminutive 0-4-0 Saddle Tank was built by Peckett & Sons in 1915 and originally worked at the Heap Bridge Paper Mill near Bury. This setting depicts the loco against a fine renovated signal gantry on 6 April 2009.

Although most locos were kept at Buckley Wells, there was a small shed to the north of the station at Castlecroft. On 25 June 1995 preserved Deltic Class 55 No. D9015 *Tulyar* (55015) and Class 30 Sulzer No. D5518 (31101), both in original BR colours, were in residence whilst Ivatt 2-6-0 No. 46441 drifted by light engine.

An unusual visitor to the ELR was this Derby Lightweight two-car battery-driven BMU comprising coaches Nos 79998 and 79999. New in April 1958, it was transferred into departmental use in October 1967 in which guise it remained until 1985. It was photographed at Burrs on 6 June 1993 having formed the 09.10 Rawtenstall to Bury working. In 2023 it was based on home ground at the Royal Deeside Railway at Banchory having first entered service from Kittybrewster MPD sixty-five years earlier.

The East Lancashire Railway hosted all types of preserved locos, both steam and diesel. Having just left Summerseat on 8 January 1993 with the 10.00 departure from Bury, Castle Class 4-6-0 No. 5029 *Nunney Castle* presents an explosive sight in the clear cold winter atmosphere. Built at Swindon in 1934, the privately owned Castle was renovated to main line standards in 1990 whilst based at the Didcot Railway Centre. Its status in 2021 saw it under overhaul at Locomotive Services Ltd at Crewe.

The Midland 0-6-0 4F was a versatile loco and was quite content pulling heavy coal trains or seaside bound excursions. Of the 580 engines built from 1922 to 1941 just three survived into preservation. Normally based at the Churnet Valley Railway the 'Midi' was photographed crossing Brooksbottom Viaduct at Summerseat, complete with yellow cabside stripe, with a demonstration freight train on 29 January 2006.

The former ELR was officially closed completely by BR in March 1982. However, the ELR reopened the line as far as Ramsbottom on 25 July 1987 to run its newly inaugurated heritage service. Long-time preserved and home-based Western hydraulic No. D1041 *Western Prince* was recorded at Ramsbottom with a Bury to Rawtenstall train on 16 June 1991. Built at Crewe in 1962, the loco was withdrawn by BR in February 1977.

The line was further extended to Rawtenstall in 1991. Preserved Class 50 No. 50015 (D415) *Valiant* was photographed approaching Ramsbottom station on 6 June 1993 with the 11.30 Rawtenstall to Bury Bolton Street. The Class 50 was withdrawn by BR in June 1992 and is based at the ELR. Ramsbottom Station Signal Box was opened by the LMS on 25 May 1938.

The Somerset & Dorset Joint Railway took delivery from Derby Works of six Fowler 2-8-0 7Fs in 1914. These were followed by a further five in 1925 from RSH, two of which are preserved. Number 53809 was photographed at Ewood Bridge on 17 October 1992 with the 10.00 Bury to Rawtenstall. The locomotive was privately owned in 2023 and was based at the North Norfolk Railway.

One hundred and one Hymek diesel hydraulic locos were built at Beyer Peacock's Gorton factory between 1961and 1964. These were some of the last locos built there before the works closed. The last of the type remained in service until early 1975, which included three of the four preserved examples, Nos D7017/8/29. The fourth example that was saved for posterity was No. D7076, which was withdrawn by BR in May 1973 and is seen at Townsend Fold on 11 June 1994 with the 15.30 Rawtenstall to Bury. The signal box dates from 1959.

Rawtenstall was reached by the ELR in 1991 and is the northern terminus of the line. However, in BR days it was a through station with the line continuing on to Bacup; this latter section was closed by BR in December 1966. Warship Class 42 No. D832 *Onslaught* was turned out of Swindon Works in February 1961; withdrawn by BR in December 1972, it was one of only two Warships to survive into preservation. It is seen arriving at Rawtenstall with a rake of inappropriate NSE-liveried Mark II coaches in tow on 11 June 1994 with the 14.00 from Bury.

BRC&W Class 104 DMU Nos 53512 and 53460 is seen alongside Miles Platting Junction Signal Box on 1 October 1985 with the 10.00 Manchester Victoria to Oldham via Rochdale and Shaw. Miles Platting station was closed on 27 May 1995 with the signal box following on 4 August 1998. In the distance is Class 47 No. 47426 (D1534), climbing the bank with an unidentified special working. Number 53512 was later paired with No. 53431 and the 104 set was condemned in 1990.

Class 37 No. 37891 (D6866) was photographed from Clegg Hall Road at Smithy Bridge on the Caldervale line in charge of 6E25, the Stanlow to Leeds tanker train on 13 July 1993. The line was opened by the Manchester & Leeds Railway as far as Littleborough on 3 July 1839.

Preserved Duchess Class Pacific No. 46229 *Duchess of Hamilton* was photographed at Ashton Moss North Junction on 30 March 1996 with 'The Trans Pennine Express' railtour from Preston to Scarborough (and return). The signal box was closed on 14 April 2018 and the junction (with the line leading to the Guide Bridge to Stockport line) was later remodelled.

The twenty-three-arch rock-faced stone Saddleworth Viaduct was built in 1849 and crosses the River Tame and the Huddersfield Narrow Canal, as well as a number of roads. Class 47 No. 47596 (D1933) *Aldeburgh Festival* is seen in charge of a RES Parcels train heading for Manchester on 20 July 1993. The canal can be seen at the bottom of the valley passing under a 'skewed arch'. Lock No. 23 of 74 is just visible under the arch.

The line then continues on towards Diggle and Standedge. Diggle Junction was where two separate lines from Stalybridge converged, one via Uppermill, which closed in 1966, and the other via Mossley. Diggle Junction Signal Box was opened in 1885 and was still functioning in 2024. Super Sprinter No. 158807 is seen on 20 July 1993 with the 09.22 Liverpool Lime Street to Newcastle Central.

Also seen approaching Diggle Junction on 20 July 1993 is Pacer unit No. 142069 with the 08.55 Manchester Victoria to Wakefield Westgate. The village of Saddleworth is in the background. The tall building (clock tower) on the left was part of the W. H. Shaw Loom Works, which was built in 1860 and latterly was home to a wooden pallet works. It was demolished in 2015 and the site is now occupied by a new school.

Super Sprinter No. 158768 has just emerged from the west portal of the 5,675-yard-long Standedge tunnel on 20 July 1993. It is working the 08.30 Wakefield Westgate to Manchester Victoria. Pacer car No. 55640 of unit No. 142049 is about to enter the tunnel. There were in fact four separate tunnels, two each carrying a single line, which were opened in 1848 and 1871 and are now closed (these were on the right), a canal tunnel and a double-track tunnel, which was opened in 1894. It is the latter which is currently in use. This was also the site of Diggle station, which closed on 7 October 1968.

Guide Bridge station was opened by the SA&MR on 11 November 1841 and at one time had lines radiating out to all four points of the compass. At its maximum it had four through platforms and boasted extensive siding space. Now reduced to two platforms, it still plays host to a large Network Rail Engineering Depot. On 12 June 1993 Sprinters Nos 158749 and 158901 pass non-stop with trains to Scarborough and Manchester respectively. In 2025 the station was mainly served by the Hadfield and Rose Hill services.

Once a busy place with freight trains using the Woodhead route, such traffic diminished with its closure. On 12 June 1993 Class 56 No. 56027 pilots Class 47 No. 47378 (D1897) on a train of freightliner flats, which have just joined the main line from the Stockport direction. The classic timber and slate roof footbridge was demolished following an arson attack in October 2006.

Electric trains finally commenced running on the Woodhead line in September 1954. A system using 1500v dc overhead collection was used. Eight three-car EMU sets were especially built at BRC&W to work the local trains as far as Hadfield. Class 506 Set No. 007 is seen at Dinting (reduced to one platform) with a train from Hadfield to Manchester Piccadilly on 26 March 1981.

Another view recorded on 26 March 1981 depicts Class 76s Nos 76007 (E26007) and 76012 (E26012) with a rake of loaded mineral wagons heading towards Mottram Sidings. The Down line was taken out of use following a freight train derailment on 10 March. Dinting Station Signal Box was opened by the GCR in 1905 and was still functioning in 2025. The line was closed to freight on 18 July 1981. Only No. E26020 survives in preservation.

The Class 506s survived until the end of 1984 when they were finally withdrawn after thirty years service. The line to Hadfield was re-energised at 25kv ac and the service was taken over by EMUs of classes 303–305. Class 304 No. 304015 is seen at the single-platform Glossop station on 12 June 1993 with the 12.08 from Hadfield to Manchester Piccadilly. The Hadfield trains made the detour into Glossop station in both directions of travel.

An unidentified Hadfield EMU set is seen in the rugged landscape approaching Dinting with a Hadfield bound train on 26 March 1981. These units were maintained at Reddish Depot before closure in May 1983 and then Longsight, to which location they had to be towed. Looks like the local football match might have had to be cancelled due to a broken crossbar.

Hadfield set No. 006 presents a forlorn sight at Hadfield on 11 December 1976. Notice how the platform has only been swept as far as the first set of doors on the leading coach. These units were all scrapped at Vic Berry's Leicester scrap yard in 1985. This is now the end of the line.

In happier times Class 76s Nos 76021 (E26021) and 76008 (E26008) were photographed at Hadfield on 26 March 1981 with a train of loaded MGRs bound for Fiddlers Ferry Power Station. Hadfield Signal Box only dated from March 1964 but was closed in December 1984 when the line was converted to 25kv ac energy collection. Saddleworth Moor forms the backdrop.

On 29 December 1976 Class 76s Nos 76033 (E26033) and 76015 (E26015) were photographed passing Bottoms Reservoir just beyond Hadfield with a mineral train bound for South Yorkshire. The reservoir was one of a series constructed between 1865 and 1877 to supply water from the River Etherow to the Manchester conurbation.

Rose Hill (Marple) became a terminus station when the line beyond to Macclesfield was closed on 5 January 1970 with the closure of High Lane, Higher Poynton and Bollington stations. The line had been opened by the Manchester, Bollington & Marple Railway on 2 August 1869. In 2025 a basic hourly service was provided to/from Manchester Piccadilly via Guide Bridge. This was also the case in 1993 when Pacer No. 142034 was pictured at the single platform on 12 June with the 11.20 return to Manchester.

On 18 September 1994 Pathfinder Tours ran a series of railtours under the banner of 'The Lancastrians', which used no fewer than twelve different locos. After a run from Piccadilly to the Bredbury Waste Terminal and back the tour again left Piccadilly behind Class 31s Nos 31160 (D5578) and 31427 (D5618) bound for Rose Hill via Reddish North and Brinnington. The train is seen heading away from the camera at Redhouse Lane with Class 56 No. 56056 trailing.

New Mills Central station (originally New Mills) was opened by the Manchester, Sheffield & Lincolnshire Railway on 1 July 1865. A short branch was opened to Hayfield in January 1868 but this was closed in January 1970. The line beyond New Mills was opened by the Midland Railway in the mid-1860s. On 3 July 1984 Class 31 No. 31427 (D5618) had paused at the station with the 12.10 Hull Paragon to Manchester Piccadilly.

As the line leaves New Mills towards Chinley it crosses over the River Sett in a deep gorge. A Class 108 DMU, which has formed the 13.38 from Manchester Piccadilly to Sheffield stopping service, can be seen high above the river on 3 July 1984. The viaduct dates from 1864 to 1865.

Following the demise of steam the Tunstead to Northwich limestone trains were worked by a variety of motive power including Classes 20, 25, 37, 40, 45 and 47. Twin-headcode Class 40 No. 40143 (D343) is seen passing under the Hyde Bank Road road bridge on 3 July 1984 as it heads east through New Mills with a rake of empty hoppers bound for Peak Forest. The Class 40 was withdrawn in January 1985 and cut up at Crewe the following year.

1985 was the year of introduction of the new generation of DMUs in the form of ninety-six Class 142 Pacer units, with the first fourteen being allocated to the Manchester area. Painted in GMPTE colours, brand new No. 142001 was photographed at New Mills on 19 June 1985 on a test outing. It is full of BR personnel wearing hi-viz vests with a pile of white-coloured sacks visible behind the front entrance.

Another empty limestone train was photographed at New Mills South Junction on 27 December 1984 behind Class 20s Nos 20070 (D8070) and 20159 (D8159). In the 1970s these trains were operated by a pool of seven Class 25s which were based at Trafford Park MPD (9E), with the train usually extending to eighteen wagons. The signal box was opened in 1903 and was still open in 2025.

Class 47 No. 47327 (D1808) is seen on the outskirts of New Mills with the 10.09 Barrow-in-Furness to Nottingham on 3 July 1984. This was one of the slow-speed Type 4s which were not fitted with a heating boiler and would only have been seen on passenger workings in the summer. It was cut up at C. F. Booth's Rotherham scrap yard in November 1993.

On 19 June 1985 Brush Type 4 No. 47100 (D1687) was photographed crossing the River Goyt thirteen-arch stone viaduct at New Mills with a cement train from Earles Sidings at Hope. The train may have been heading for the Blue Circle Cement depot at Northenden. This section of line was opened by the Midland Railway in 1904. The nearside line was out of use and the train is running wrong line.

Class 101 DMU Nos 51230 and 54056 was photographed approaching Chinley station on 26 June 1994 with what purported to be a local train from Edale to Stockport. This section of the line had clearly been four-track in the past to cater for the intense cement and stone traffic from the nearby industrial complexes.

By 1998 the passenger services on the Hope Valley line had been in the hands of Sprinters for a few years. 'Super Sprinter' No. 158774 is seen passing Edale Signal Box on 13 February with the 10.42 Manchester Airport to Cleethorpes. This train would have reversed at Manchester Piccadilly. The signal box was opened by the Midland Railway in 1893 and was still in use in 2025. The imposing slope of Kinder Scout, standing at 2,087 feet above sea level, provides the backdrop.

Class 59 No. 59201 *National Railway Museum* was the first of six of the type ordered by National Power. It was built by EMD of London, Ontario, Canada, and arrived in the UK on 17 February 1994. This lone engine was initially used to convey limestone from Peak Forest to Drax Power Station. It is seen at Edale in charge of 6E56, the 06.39 from Peak Forest on 24 June 1994. The remaining five were delivered the following August and all six were put to work on coal trains in the Aire Valley.

Seen at the same location is preserved crimson Ivatt 2-6-0 No. 46441 on 26 June 1994 with the 'Hope Valley Centenarians' railtour 1Z63 08.20 Bolton to Sheffield. Presumably the tour ran to celebrate the centenary of the opening of the line. Originally comprising a class of 128 engines, seven of the type survived into preservation.

The Midland Railway opened its main line through the limestone deposits of the Peak Forest and Derbyshire Dales in February 1867 and it remained a trunk route to Derby and onwards to London for just over a century. The line was closed beyond Millers Dale in June 1968. Class 47 No. 47532 (D1641) is seen at Peak Forest with a rake of cement wagons on 17 May 1990. The lone Class 37 would have been on banking duty.

Class 20s Nos 20902 (D8060) and 20903 (D8083) are seen at Peak Forest 'top and tailing' a Chapman's weedkiller train heading in the direction of New Mills. Although Peak Forest station was closed on 6 March 1967 and the platforms removed (it had three through platforms and a bay), some of the station buildings remained in situ and served as a 'signing on' point.

Quarrying for limestone has gone on for centuries in the Peak Forest district and a number of quarry sites established their own internal tramway systems in the nineteenth century. However, it was in the early 1930s when the white/grey stone began to be quarried on an industrial scale. The Buxton Lime Co. was formed in 1891; the successor of the BLC and a number of Independents was the Imperial Chemical Industries (ICI) in 1931. *Above:* Class 60 No. 60016 *Langdale Pikes* with an empty rake of Tiphook bogie hoppers is seen at the RMC (Ready Mixed Concrete) quarry site on 28 July 1993. This site was acquired by the Mexican conglomerate CEMEX in 2005. *Below:* Seen at the same location but heading for the Tunstead ICI quarry on 19 June 1996 are Class 37s Nos 37415 (D6977) and 37426 (D6999). The wagons in this train are positively antiquarian compared to the Tiphooks. Class 60 No. 60097 *Pillar* and Class 08 No. 08915 (D4145) are in the RMC sidings.

Back in the 1960s the sleek Midland Pullman would have sped through this industrial landscape. Thirty years later and with the line curtailed beyond Millers Dale, the remaining section now only saw freight train movements. On 2 February 1997 Class 37s Nos 37671 (D6947) *Tre Pol and Pen* and 37509 (D6793) were photographed at Great Rocks Junction with a train of empty stone wagons bound for the nearby Tunstead ICI Aggregates complex. Longsiding Lime Works used to occupy the hill area on the right and is believed to have been closed in the late 1930s.

Prominent in this picture, which dates from 19 July 1993, are the limekilns of Tarmac's Tunstead Concrete Plant which was first established on this site in the 1920s. The track leads down to the extensive quarry site. Class 37 No. 37520 (D6741) has been given the road to join the main line at Great Rocks Junction.

Even by the 1990s there was still the need for a diesel shunter at Peak Forest. These would be maintained at nearby Buxton MPD. On 27 November 1994 Class 08 No. 08911 (D4141) was resting outside the shed building. It was built at Horwich Works in 1962 and is now part of the NRM collection and carries the name *Matey*.

Steam finished at Buxton MPD in January 1968 and a new two road maintenance depot was built to accommodate the modern order. On 1 August 1991 Class 37s Nos 37414 (D6987) and 37678 (D6956) were standing sentry. At the side is an unidentified Class 31 and Class 122 Route Learning single car DMU No. 01 (TDB975023), which originally carried the number W55001. It was built by the Gloucester RC&W Co. and delivered new to Reading MPD in May 1958. It was withdrawn from Longsight in 1996 and is now preserved at the East Lancashire Railway. Buxton TMD has long since been demolished.

On Sunday 11 April 1993 Class 60s Nos 60096 *Ben Macdui* and 60015 *Bow Fell* were residing in Buxton station alongside Sprinter No. 150142. This was now the new order for some of the stone trains out of Peak Forest. Both locos were still serviceable in 2023. Both the LNWR and MR reached Buxton in 1863 and a joint station was opened on 15 June.

In the early 1990s many of the trains from Manchester to Buxton originated in West Lancashire, which was made possible by the opening of the Windsor Link. On a misty 30 November 1991 Sprinter No. 150150 has paused at Chapel-en-le-Frith with the 06.15 Barrow-in-Furness to Buxton. The station was the scene of a railway disaster involving an LMS 8F on 9 February 1957 when both the driver and fireman lost their lives in an attempt to control a runaway freight train.

A little further along the line towards Manchester and on the same day Sprinter No. 150231 was photographed at Furness Vale with the 09.38 Buxton to Blackpool North. The line to Whaley Bridge had been opened by the LNWR in 1857 before being extended to Buxton six years later.

Also seen at Furness Vale on 30 November 1991 are Class 20s Nos 20057 (D8057) and 20013 (D8013), which were in charge of Pathfinder Tours 'Two Counties Crusader' railtour 1Z16, the 09.39 Manchester Piccadilly to Hindlow. The train had originated at Swindon behind Class 47 No. 47818 (D1917) at 04.55 and was due back at 21.47 but dropped around two hours on the schedule throughout the day. The signal box and associated semaphore signals were still in use in 2023.

Sprinter units Nos 150137 and 150138 are seen on the Castlefield Arches on 27 June 1993 with the 08.22 Buxton to Blackpool North. This short section of line was built by the MSJ&AR in 1849 to connect the Altrincham line to the original Manchester and Liverpool line at Ordsall Lane Junction. One of the units has been strengthened by the addition of a disbanded Class 150/2 carriage.

Another picture taken from the same vantage point at Castlefield on the same day. This photograph features Class 37s Nos 37408 (D6989) *Loch Rannoch* and 37429 (D6600) with the 09.17 SuO Crewe to Blackpool North. The cross-lattice girder bridge on the left was built by the CLC in 1892 to provide separate access for the new Deansgate Goods Depot, which was built alongside Central station. Having been devoid of tracks for several decades it was being incorporated into a linear park/landscaped open space in 2022.

The Ordsall Chord was opened on 10 December 2017 and enabled trains to run directly between Victoria and Piccadilly stations for the first time. The centrepiece of this short section of railway is this curved bow-arch suspension bridge, which was specially designed and built to span the River Irwell. TransPennine Class 185 No. 185132 is seen on the bridge on 4 July 2018 with the 10.19 Manchester Airport to Newcastle Central. In the foreground is the truncated section of MOSI's demonstration line.

The original Liverpool Road station was a remarkable survivor. It ceased to be used as a passenger station in May 1844 but was converted for use as a goods depot, in which guise it continued to be used until 1975. The station building and adjacent historic railway warehouses now form part of the Museum of Science & Industry (MOSI). A special event was held on 2 August 1980 to commemorate its 150th anniversary. One of the attendees was preserved ex-LMS 0-6-0T Jinty No. 7298.

Also present on the same day was a replica of Stephenson's *Rocket*, which was employed to give rides in a matching replica carriage on a short length of track. The original *Rocket* was built on Tyneside in 1829 for the Liverpool & Manchester Railway. Following display at the Science Museum in London it was moved to the NRM in 2018.

EWS Class 66 No. 66059 is viewed from Deansgate tram station with an eastbound liner train from Trafford Park FLT on 8 September 2011. It is crossing Castle Street Bridge as it approaches Deansgate railway station. In the background is Beetham Tower, which was a feature of the Knott Mill Congregational Church, which was completed in 1853 and is a Grade II listed building.

Deansgate station was originally known as Knott Mill & Deansgate and was opened by the MSJ&AR on 20 July 1849. Mersey Travel-liveried Sprinter No. 150211 waits in platform 1 on 11 July 1993 with the 08.35 Wigan Wallgate to Alderley Edge.

Twenty-two years later FLHH Class 70 No. 70009 was photographed hauling 4L90, the 10.20 Trafford Park FLT to Felixstowe liner train. Freightliner operated twenty of these distinctive looking locos, which were built by GE at their Erie Plant in Pennsylvania and first introduced into service in July 2009. No. 70009 was working on loan to Colas Rail in 2024.

A number of services from Wales to Manchester were operated by Coradia Class 175/0 and 175/1 DMUs. They were built by Alstom at Washwood Heath and first introduced in 1999. Seen during its time with Arriva Trains Wales at Oxford Road on 17 July 2013 is set No. 175102, which is working 1H88, the 12.53 Llandudno Junction to Manchester Airport. Operation of these units was transferred to 'Transport for Wales Rail' in February 2021 and they were retired from service by the operator in 2024. A diverted Voyager train is receding into the distance.

Oxford Road station was also opened by the MSJ&AR on 20 July 1849. It was extensively refurbished in 1960 with the use of timber featuring prominently – these timber-constructed features are now Grade II listed. The Class 128 Gloucester RC&W Co.-built DMU was a purpose-built single car unit first introduced in 1959 to convey parcels traffic. There were ten units in the class, which were evenly distributed between the WR and LMR. Now painted in Post Office red, No. 55992 was photographed at Oxford Road on 27 October 1989 and has possibly originated from Chester. Note the wooden canopy.

The station was originally built with just two through platforms and two dead-end stabling roads on the eastern approach. It was expanded over the years to a maximum size of four through platforms and two bays on the northern side at the western end; there were two stabling roads between the bays. Over the years the bays have been used by the Altrincham electric service and the special train service to Manchester United's Old Trafford ground. Only one bay was in use in 2025. On 17 July 2013 FLHH Class 66 No. 66516 is seen passing through platform 2 with 4L18, the 14.20 Trafford Park to Felixstowe liner train.

The footbridge was a later addition to the station and at the time of this photograph it had not long since been refurbished. Demonstrating the flexibility of bi-directional running, Class 92 No. 92032 *César Franck I Mech E Railway Division* was travelling westbound through platform 2 on 17 July 2013 with 4M18 from Felixstowe to Trafford Park FLT. GBRF operated just four of these underused machines.

TPE Class 185 DMU No. 185112 has stopped in platform 4 on 24 November 2020 with 1P72, the 11.51 Saltburn to Manchester Airport, which has travelled via Manchester Victoria and the Ordsall Chord. The Northern unit visible on the left is waiting in the one remaining bay, platform 5, with a train for either Warrington or Liverpool.

Oxford Road in Manchester was reputed to be the second busiest bus corridor in the UK, after Oxford Street in London. Immediately on leaving Oxford Road station the line crossed over this nondescript looking bridge. However, the bridge is actually fabricated out of cast iron with rib-girders and is encased in concrete. The concrete was completely renewed in 2009. The leading coach of East Midlands Trains' Sprinter No. 158812 sits astride the bridge as it proceeds on its journey from Liverpool Lime Street to Norwich on 27 September 2017 whilst Stagecoach buses pass underneath.

Between Castlefield and Fairfield the two-track line is carried on a long series of red-brick arches interspersed with a number of iron bridges. Presiding over the line is the Kimpton Clock Tower, which was built in three stages between 1891 and 1932. Class 37 No. 37515 (D6764) is seen on 29 March 1991 squeezing between the buildings, none of which would have existed when the line was built, with a return empty tanker train from Glazebrook to Lindsey on Humberside.

Tyseley-based Class 117 DMU Nos 51370, 59522 and 51412 was photographed on the arches with an ECS working on 29 March 1991. The trainshed roof of Manchester Piccadilly station is just visible on the right. The vantage point for these two pictures was a multistorey car park.

The Class 304 (AM4) EMUs were specifically built for the newly electrified north-west lines centred on Crewe and Manchester. Forty-five sets were constructed at BR's Wolverton Works between 1959 and 1962; they were operated as either three- or four-car sets. Number 304012 was photographed approaching platform 13 at Piccadilly with the 13.05 Altrincham to Crewe on 1 June.

Ninety-one Class 303 (AM3) EMUs, originally known as 'Blue Trains', were built by Pressed Steel at Linwood in Ayrshire in 1959–61 to operate the Glasgow suburban network. By 1981 thirteen sets were deemed surplus to requirements and transferred to the Manchester area. Number 303067 is seen at platform 13 at Piccadilly on 1 June 1985 with the 12.50 Altrincham to Alderley Edge via Styal. All were repainted in the PTE orange and brown livery, with the last of the sets being withdrawn in 1993.

What is now Manchester Piccadilly station was first opened by the M&BR as Store Street on 8 May 1842. It was also used by the M&SR, which shared its tracks from Ardwick Junction. Within a few years the station expanded and was renamed London Road. It later reached its maximum size of twelve bay and two through platforms and was extensively rebuilt in the late 1950s as part of the WCML electrification and modernisation programme. It was renamed again as Piccadilly in 1960. Platforms 1 to 4, which are on view here, were electrified in 1954 as part of the Woodhead route electrification scheme. Sprinter No. 158753 and Class 108 Nos 53971 and 54504 were on view on 30 May 1992.

The last of the Class 85s lingered on until the end of 1991, with some of the last duties being to haul empty stock trains into/out of London Euston and Manchester Piccadilly stations. Seen on 23 October 1989, No. 85030 (E3085) was employed on such a duty. Originally classified AL5, No. E3085 was turned out of Doncaster Works in July 1964. It was withdrawn in September 1990 and cut up at MC Metals in Glasgow two years later.

Built by BR at their York and Wolverton Works, the Class 309s entered service in 1962 working longer-distance trains on the GEML out of Liverpool Street. As such they attained the name of Clacton Units. Surplus to requirements by 1994, seven of the twenty-three sets were transferred to Longsight for use on some of the medium-distance trains out of Piccadilly. Number 309616, in NSE livery, was being used for driver training on 25 March 1994. They remained in service until late 2000. The impressive glass/steel station canopy roof is made up of four adjacent connected parallel straight sections.

Two intending lady passengers are chatting away underneath the nameplate of *The Girls' Brigade*, which was attached to Class 90 No. 90002. The loco was named at London Euston on 6 April 1993 and renamed *Mission Impossible* on 10 March 1997. The Girls' Brigade was formed in 1965 as an amalgamation of The Girls' Brigade (Ireland), The Girls' Guildry (Scotland) and The Girls' Life Brigade (England).

Two photos taken in quick succession on 17 June 1994. *Above:* Class 56 No. 56065 has briefly stopped at platform 13 to change drivers with the British Tar Products' tanker train from Glazebrook to Lindsey. An unidentified Class 158 Sprinter is waiting to depart platform 14 with a train for Liverpool Lime Street. *Below:* A number of the Class 305/4 EMUs were also transferred north to Longsight. Numbers 305420/410 are about to reverse back into the station having just set forward and will form a train to Hazel Grove. Both of these three-car sets are in different liveries. On the far right No. 305510, in the GMPTE livery, has just departed with a train for Hadfield. The tail end of the tanker train on the right completes the picture. Out of sight on the right was the site of Manchester Mayfield station, which was closed in November 1960 having latterly been used as an overspill during the reconstruction of London Road/Piccadilly.

Two pictures which illustrate the variety of multiple units that were providing the local services in the late 1990s. *Above:* On 29 October 1997 a somewhat grubby-looking EMU No. 305507 is waiting at platform 4 with a train for 'well who knows where'. Adjacent in platform 3 is Sprinter No. 158767, which is bound for Cleethorpes, then in platform 2 Class 101 DMU Nos 51426 and 54358 is waiting to depart for Rose Hill and finally in platform 1 is a Class 323 EMU on the Hadfield service. *Below:* Also seen on the Hadfield service on 18 February 1998 is Class 323 EMU No. 323233, but this one in now displaying the 'north western trains' livery; Class 101 DMU Set No. 101658 is occupying platform 2. The 323s were built by Hunslet Transportation between 1992 and 1995, with the first eventually entering service in February 1994. Forty-three sets were constructed, of which seventeen were allocated to the north-west. Operated by Northern Trains in 2025, they were maintained at Allerton TMD. The original Store Street station was on the opposite side of the wall.

With the dawn of the twenty-first century and long after the variety of steam, diesel and electric locos which had graced the station over the previous five decades had been consigned to the history books came the Virgin revolution. Latterly electric locos of Classes 86/2, 87 and 90 had been in charge of the cross-country and London bound trains but these were gradually replaced from July 2002 onwards by Richard Branson's fleet of electric Pendolinos and diesel-powered Voyagers. *Above:* Three Class 390 Pendolinos are depicted in this view, which was recorded on 16 June 2010; at one time trains left for London Euston every twenty minutes. The WCML franchise was taken over by Avanti West Coast in December 2019 using the same rebranded trains. *Below:* The Voyager fleet was split between the West Coast and Cross Country services. The Class 220/221s were of either four- or five-car formation and often worked in pairs. On 4 March 2013 Set No. 220016 was waiting to depart with a service for the south-west, possibly Reading or Bournemouth. Class 323 EMU No. 323235 can be seen on a local train.

The first engine shed on the Longsight site was opened by the M&BR in 1842. It was a modest affair with a small octagonal shed, a separate shed and a carriage shed. Over the years it has been redeveloped several times and has catered for steam, diesel and electric locomotives and multiple units. In 2025 the depot was managed by Alstom and was home to Avanti West Coast's fleet of Pendolinos. In 1992 the TMD celebrated 150 years of continuous operation with a public open day. A number of preserved engines were on display. *Above:* Representing two steam types that could have had a previous association with the depot were Riddles Standard Pacific No. 71000 *Duke of Gloucester* and Stanier Black 5 4-6-0 No. 45305 *Alderman A E Draper*. *Below:* Preserved diesels in attendance included Crompton No. 33008 (D6508) *Eastleigh*, Class 50 No. 50017 *Royal Oak* (D417) and Deltic No. 55015 (D9015) *Tulyar*, the last of which is pictured below.

Seen inside Longsight TMD on 26 April 1992, on the occasion of the open day, are Class 37 No. 37070 (D6770) and Class 47 No. 47053 (D1635). The latter carried the names *Impala* (in 1990) and *Cory Brothers 1842–1992* (in 1992). It is presumed that the planters were not a permanent feature.

The Manchester & Birmingham Railway opened the last section of its line between Stockport and Manchester Store Street in May 1842. Over the years there were three intermediate stations situated at Heaton Norris (1840–1959), Heaton Chapel and Levenshulme. Class 101 DMU Nos 53164, 59539 and 53160 is seen passing through the latter on 29 November 1994 heading towards Piccadilly. It had recently been repainted into the green heritage livery.

Levenshulme was a simple two-platform station on a four-track main line. *Above:* On 22 May 1993 large-logo Class 47 No. 47443 (D1559) *North Eastern* was photographed heading towards Piccadilly with an unidentified train. The author first remembers seeing this loco in March 1964 at Preston on a test run from Crewe Works to Penrith. It was withdrawn in October 1993 and cut up at Crewe Works three years later. *Below:* Class 37 No. 37429 (D6600) *Eisteddfod Genedlaethol* and Class 31 No. 31421 (D5558) *Wigan Pier* are in charge of the 07.53 SuO Crewe to Blackpool North on 5 September 1993 as they head towards Piccadilly. Levenshulme had previously boasted another station on the nearby MS&LR line (the Fallowfield loop from Chorlton-cum-Hardy to Guide Bridge), which was renamed Levenshulme South; it was opened on 2 May 1892 and closed on 7 July 1958, although the line remained open for freight and other movements until 1987. The impressive station building fronting Stockport Road was still standing in 2023.

The station was largely rebuilt (simplified) in 1959 in conjunction with the Crewe to Manchester electrification scheme. The works included demolition of some of the platform buildings and renewal of the platforms using concrete segments to replace the previous wooden structures. In 2025 it was served variously by Piccadilly stopping trains to/from Alderley Edge, Buxton, Crewe and Hazel Grove. Class 304 EMU No. 040 was heading for Stoke-on-Trent on 2 January 1993 whilst No. 010 has just departed with a train for Manchester.

Porterbrook was a rolling stock leasing company which was established in March 1994 as part of the privatisation process. A handful of locos were painted in their house colours of purple and white. Seen at Levenshulme working for Virgin Cross Country on 8 March 1997 is Class 47 No. 47817 (D1611) hauling the 09.17 SuO Manchester Piccadilly to London Paddington. The Class 47 was later reincarnated as Class 57 No. 57311 *Parker* in the Virgin Thunderbird Pool.

Just 1.4 miles further east of Levenshulme is situated Heaton Chapel station. It was opened by the LNWR in 1852 and has been providing a local service to Stockport and Manchester ever since. Class 90 No. 90007 was photographed racing through on 2 May 1995 with the 13.00 London Euston to Manchester Piccadilly. Note the distinctive footbridge which regrettably was removed in the mid-2000s.

The station was originally called Heaton Chapel and Heaton Moor but the name was shortened in the late 1950s. The main line from Manchester to Stockport was quadrupled during the 1880s and the electrification works were completed in September 1960. A mother and her young son look on as Pacer unit No. 142060 whizzes through with a Southport to Chester train on 5 August 1995.

Heaton Chapel only sees a small amount of freight pass through and these mainly consist of liner trains. Class 90 No. 90130 *Fretconnection*, in a special rendition of the SNCF livery, was photographed heading for Trafford Park FLT on 17 September 1994. The diminutive Heaton Chapel and Heaton Moor Signal Box, which was only equipped with twelve levers, used to stand between the two pairs of tracks on the left but was swept away with the electrification works.

Super power was provided for the 06.45 London Euston to Manchester Piccadilly on 17 September 1994, which is seen drifting through Heaton Chapel on the slow line behind Class 86 No. 86224 *Caledonian* and Class 90 No. 90012 *Royal Anglian Regiment*.

In 1993 many Cross Country services were being worked by HSTs. Storming through the centre Road at Heaton Chapel on 27 March were Nos 43071 and 43062 with the 08.18 Manchester Piccadilly to Bournemouth. The HSTs were first introduced in 1976 and proved to be one of the most successful designs operated in the modern era. In 2025 No. 43071 was preserved whilst No. 43062 had joined the Network Rail fleet.

The line from Stockport to Guide Bridge was opened by the Manchester & Birmingham Railway in October 1845. There were just two stations on the 5-mile-long line at Reddish South and Denton. The normal weekday service was one of the sparsest in the country with just one departure each week on a Friday from Stockport with no return. Class 37 No. 37414 (D6987) *Cathays C&W Works 1846–1993* has just passed through Reddish South with a special working towards Guide Bridge on 8 May 1993.

Seen at the same location on the same day is Class 101 DMU Nos 51442 and 54061, which is not in passenger service. Although this line has no passenger service, so to speak, it is used by a number of freight trains. Now reduced to a single face, Reddish South station did at one time have four through platforms.

Class 87 No. 87010 *King Arthur* was photographed arriving at Stockport with the 09.30 Manchester Piccadilly to London Euston on 20 March 1993. It has just crossed the twenty-seven -arch red-brick viaduct, which was opened by the Manchester & Birmingham Railway and was completed in December 1840. Originally it accommodated two tracks but was widened to carry four in 1887–89.

After a period of using a temporary station (Heaton Norris) on the north side of the River Mersey Valley for over two years, the larger Stockport station was opened by the M&BR on 15 February 1843. Class 86/2 No. 86228 (E3167) *Vulcan Heritage* waits to depart platform 2 with the 14.18 Manchester Piccadilly to Birmingham International on 17 July 1993. Just visible above the end of the train is Stockport No.1 Signal Box, which was opened by the LNWR in 1884. It was still in use in 2025.

Seen at the same platform but at the north end (loco pushing) is VT-liveried Class 90 No. 90002 *Mission Impossible* (previously named *Girls' Brigade* – see p. 63) with the 13.30 Manchester Piccadilly to London Euston. Stockport is one of only nine stations in the UK that has a platform 0. These are usually additional platforms which have been added without renumbering the station's other platforms.

Stabled alongside Stockport station on 6 February 1994 were Class 304 EMU units Nos 304032 and 304009. These first generation electric units were initially painted in BR green with thin yellow lines above and below the windows and the lion and wheel emblem. This livery was superseded by all-over 'Rail Blue' in the late 1960s. The blue and white 'Provincial' colour scheme was introduced in the mid-1970s. Then followed Regional Railways blue and grey and Greater Manchester PTE brown and white.

A broadside view of Stockport's impressive brick viaduct, which carries the railway over the River Mersey Valley. An unidentified Class 40 is seen high up with a cartic train, possibly carrying Ford cars from Garston on Merseyside. The wagons are in permanently coupled sets of four and were built in the 1960s. The side screens were a later addition to protect the cars from acts of vandalism. An assortment of GMT buses can be seen below. Daw Bank bus garage is visible through the arches.

On Sunday 6 February 1994 the 11.30 Manchester Piccadilly to London Euston was in the hands of diesel power in the form of RES-liveried Class 47 No. 47588 (D1773) *Resurgent*, thereby signifying that a diversionary route might have been in the offing. Class 86 No. 86208 (E3141) *City of Chester* was on the trailing end of this train seen at Stockport.

Alderley Edge is a common destination on local Manchester trains and was served by the Class 304 EMUs for nigh on thirty-five years. The station was opened by the Manchester & Birmingham Railway on 11 May 1842 and has a modest two-platform layout with a number of nearby stabling roads. Class 304 No. 304042 is seen on 19 July 1993 with the 10.04 Crewe to Manchester Deansgate.

Mauldeth Road is situated on the line to Manchester Airport and Holmes Chapel via Styal, which was opened by the LNWR in 1909. It was one of the first sections of line to be electrified under the WCML modernisation scheme. Class 31 No. 31421 (D5558) *Wigan Pier* was photographed heading north through the station on 13 June 1993 with the diverted (via Alderley Edge and the Styal line) retimed 09.17 SuO Crewe to Blackpool North, which was normally routed via Stockport.

Manchester Airport station was opened in May 1993. It originally consisted of just two platforms; a third was added in 2008 and a fourth in 2014 when the Metrolink platforms were also constructed. A batch of nineteen Class 305/5 EMUs was built at BR York for the Liverpool Street Outer-Suburban services in 1960. These were transferred north in the early 1990s, with thirteen sets going to Manchester and five to Glasgow Shields for the North Berwick services (one unit became a Departmental in 1984). Freshly repainted and refurbished No. 305503 is waiting to depart on 12 June 1993 with the 15.10 to Piccadilly.

Manchester Airport station viewed from the terminal building. A Class 156 is paired with Class 158 No. 158749 and is seen departing platform 1 on 30 July 1994. At this time the station only comprised two platforms. A third was added on this side followed by a fourth on the opposite side, which is also where the Metrolink platforms are now located.

Sprinter unit No. 150205 was photographed at Northenden Junction on 28 July 1993 with the 14.58 Chester to Southport. The train would have travelled via Northwich, Altrincham, Stockport, Manchester, Salford Crescent and Wigan Wallgate. Class 37 No. 37417 (D6969) *Highland Region* is waiting for the road on the single line from Hazel Grove with a Northwich-bound stone train. Northenden Waste Disposal Depot is on the right.

Cromptons Nos 33025 (D6543) *Sultan* and 33116 (D6535) *Hertfordshire Rail Tours* are seen at the same location on 28 January 1995. They are working Pathfinder Tours' 'The Gladstone Bag' Railtour 1Z27 from Bristol Temple Meads to Chester via Birmingham, Derby and Chinley. Both locomotives were still extant in 2025.

In the early 1990s Northenden was still a relatively busy place. On 25 July 1993 Class 31 No. 31432 (D5571) was photographed in charge of the 09.55 Manchester Oxford Road to Llandudno. This was a Sundays only working. The Brush Type 2 was withdrawn in May 1996 and cut up at the EWS Depot at Wigan Springs Branch.

The Blue Circle Cement Depot at Northenden functioned for at least forty years, if not longer. It was established on the site of Northenden Goods Depot. Class 60 No. 60016 *Langdale Pikes* has hooked up to the wagons and will take the train the short distance to Partington as seen on 28 July 1993. Back in the 1970s this would have been a Class 25 working with a train of Prestflos. The depot latterly served as a stone terminal. Just visible in front of the bridge in the distance is Northenden Junction Signal Box, which dates from *c.* 1881 and was still functioning in 2025.

The passenger service on the former CLC route from Stockport to Warrington via Northenden was withdrawn on 30 November 1964. Northenden station had been situated just beyond the diesel unit. The cement depot then occupied what used to be a small goods depot. Pacer unit No. 142043 was working the 15.00 Southport to Chester on 28 July 1993.

Again on 28 July 1993 two eastbound freights were recorded in quick succession at Northenden. *Above:* Class 47 No. 47354 (D1835) is in charge of a short chemical train which is heading towards Hazel Grove. *Below:* Class 60 No. 60084 *Cross Fell* is approaching journey's end with the empty binliner from Warrington to Northenden Waste Disposal Depot. At the time the GMCA operated four such depots located at Bredbury, Dean Lane, Northenden and Pendleton. This line was built by the Cheshire Lines Committee in 1866 and was an important passenger route in its day, enabling trains from West Lancashire to travel to Stockport and beyond without passing through the congested environs of Manchester.

The limestone trains to/from Tunstead were often in the hands of pairs of Class 37s and usually ran seven days a week. On Sunday 1 August 1993 Nos 37417 (D6969) *Highland Region* and 37419 (D6991) are seen curving round from the Altrincham line on to the Northenden line at Skelton Junction with a train of empties.

Following the opening of the Metrolink line to Altrincham in 1992 the short section of line from Skelton Junction to Altrincham was operated as two separate single lines (one for trains and one for trams). Class 37s Nos 37421 (D6967) and 37429 (D6600) *Eisteddfod Genedlaethol* approach Navigation Road on 22 August 1993 with the 07.53 SuO Crewe to Blackpool North. A T68 tram can be seen in the distance. Note that only the tram line is electrified.

The same train is seen a week later with Class 37s Nos 37407 (D6605) *Loch Long* and 37408 (D6989) *Loch Rannoch* roaring through Altrincham station. This train was normally routed via Sandbach, Northwich, Altrincham, Stockport, Manchester Piccadilly/Oxford Road, Salford Crescent, Bolton and Preston. The imposing building is Stamford House, which was built in 1904–05 and is Grade II listed.

When the line to Altrincham was first electrified in 1931 using the 1500v dc system the local service mainly terminated at Oxford Road. The original LMS EMUs were ousted in 1971 when the line was re-electrified at 25kv ac with Class 304s providing the service. This enabled a more integrated service to be provided with trains continuing beyond Manchester to such destinations as Alderley Edge and Crewe. Units Nos 304043 and 304017 were photographed at Altrincham on 27 May 1991.

Altrincham (& Bowdon) station was opened by the MSJ&AR on 20 July 1849. The line beyond was opened by the CLC as far as Knutsford on 12 May 1862. The original EMUs were serviced in a carriage shed to the south of the station. On 12 February 1991 Class 304 No. 304042 was waiting to depart with a train for Alderley Edge whilst No. 304005 had arrived from the Manchester direction. These two platforms were reconfigured as part of the Metrolink system, which opened on 13 June 1992. The trams run on a 750v dc overhead electricity collection system.

Class 37s Nos 37075 (D6775) and 37417 (D6969) *Highland Region* were photographed on Sunday 29 August 1993 passing through Hale station with a train load of limestone bound for Oakleigh Sidings at Northwich. The limestone was used by Brunner Mond at their Winnington complex in the production of soda ash.

Another limestone train is seen a little further south at Ashley on 15 August 1993. Class 37s Nos 37405 (D6982) *Strathclyde Region* and 37430 (D6965) *Cwmbrân* have been charged with hauling this rake of fifteen wagons with a payload of 720 tons safely to Northwich. The Winnington plant rail facilities were closed in 2014 but occasional trains continued to run to the ICI terminal at nearby Lostock Graham.

Preserved Princess Pacific No. 6201 *Princess Elizabeth* was photographed approaching Northwich station on 17 June 1991 with 'The Red Rose' from Crewe to Carnforth via Chester, Manchester, Bolton and Blackburn. The Pacific was one of a class of thirteen built by the LMS at Crewe in 1933–35. The residents of the houses on the right would be hard pressed to see the railway now such is the state of the trackside growth.

Class 37 No. 37298 (D6998) is seen at Eccles on 25 April 1992 on the oldest section of railway in Manchester – the 1830-built line to Liverpool. The train is Pathfinder Tours 'Lancastrian Mini Excursion' 1T35 09.05 Crewe to Manchester Victoria. The lines on the right led to what was known as the Manchester Docks Branch. Back in the day this line served a myriad of goods facilities on the north bank of the ship canal. By 2023 just a single line served a cement depot, which at the time of writing had no scheduled rail traffic. The line through Eccles is now electrified.

Further along the original Manchester to Liverpool main line Class 45 No. 45142 (D83) was photographed at St Helens Junction on 29 May 1985 with the 12.05 Liverpool Lime Street to Scarborough. The station was opened on 15 September 1830. The Peak was built at Crewe in December 1960 and withdrawn in June 1987.

Latterly coded 9E Trafford Park Shed was located on the line to Warrington Central and Liverpool. It was built by the CLC and opened in 1895. The shed consisted of twenty dead-end roads. On 31 December 1966 the occupants consisted of forty-seven engines comprising ten Tanks, twenty-five Black 5s, ten 8Fs, one 9F, one Cl03, two Cl08, one Cl31 and one Cl40. The engine nearest to the camera is Black 5 4-6-0 No. 44851. Closure came on 4 March 1968 as steam was being eliminated by BR. The floodlights of Manchester United's Old Trafford ground can be seen beyond the shed. Part of this site is now the Trafford Park Freightliner Depot.

After passing through Trafford Park the CLC line continued through Humphrey Park, Urmston and Chassen Road before reaching Flixton. Sprinter No. 150206 was photographed there on a snowy 12 February 1991 with the 10.00 Warrington Central to Manchester Oxford Road.

Next stop along the line is Irlam, where we see vintage stock in the form of two first generation DMUs. Class 108 Nos 52058 and 51937 is Manchester bound whilst Class 101 Nos 51511 and 53853 is heading in the opposite direction – the date is 20 February 1991. Both sets have Tyseley set numbers but were based at Longsight at the time the picture was recorded. Nearby there used to be Glazebrook Exchange Sidings and the sprawling 109-acre site of Irlam Steel Works, which closed down in 1979 with the loss of 4,350 jobs.

Class 47 No. 47324 (D1807) represents a typical merry-go-round train of the 1970s. It was photographed crossing the River Mersey at Warrington Arpley on 22 February 1979 with a train of empties from Fiddlers Ferry Power Station. The Class 47/3s were fitted with slow speed control for working MGR trains. The line between Arpley and Skelton Junction was closed on 7 July 1985 and the MGR trains were rerouted via Newton-le-Willows and the Liverpool to Manchester line and through Victoria station. Arpley bus station can be seen on the right.

Freightliner Class 66 No. 66516 represents a more modern era and was photographed on the low-level line at Bank Quay on 5 June 2008 with another train of empty coal wagons from Fiddlers Ferry. The power station was decommissioned in March 2020. Opened in 1868, Warrington Bank Quay Low Level station was closed on 9 September 1963.

The first Metrolink line to open was that between Bury and Piccadilly on 6 April 1992. Through working to Altrincham followed from 15 June. Twenty-six single-articulated trams were built by Firema of Italy to initially work the system; they were fitted with four GEC motors. With No. 1009 leading this pair were photographed alongside the now more than 200-year-old Manchester Art Gallery in Mosley Street on 4 March 2013. Number 1012 had been the first of the class to be withdrawn in April 2012 whilst No. 1007 has been preserved by the Heaton Park Tramway.

The Metrolink service to Altrincham commenced on 15 June 1992 with alternate trams going through to either Piccadilly or Bury. The permanent way was shared with the railway between Altrincham and Navigation Road. Firema tram No. 1022 is seen departing Altrincham on 29 August 1993 with a service to Piccadilly. It was withdrawn in February 2014.

A further six trams were supplied by Ansaldo of Italy in December 1999 to cater for the opening of the line to Eccles. First of the batch No. 2001 is seen approaching Deansgate tram station with a service from Altrincham on 8 September 2011. These trams were also withdrawn in 2014 as the system continued to benefit from the delivery of further M5000 type trams. Deansgate station was rebuilt in 2014 with three platforms, which were located behind the photographer.

The M5000 'Flexity Swift' trams were built by Bombardier at their Bautzen factory in Germany. The first one was delivered in July 2009 followed by No. 3002 in September. The last of a protracted delivery process was No. 3147, which entered service in October 2022. The original Victoria tram stop was opened in April 1992 and consisted of a single central island with two low-level platform faces. Work to construct the line to Oldham and Rochdale took place from 2009 to 2012 and was followed by the remodelling of Victoria in 2014–15; the new arrangement had three platforms and included the provision of a spectacular curved glass/steel roof canopy. *Above:* Class leader No. 3001 with No. 3024 in tow was photographed on a service to Bury on 29 September 2015. Note the pristine cream brickwork of the back of LYR's 1909-built frontage buildings. *Below:* No. 3105 stands under the magnificent new roof on 17 August 2019 with a service from Altrincham to Bury.

No. 3071 was photographed passing the renovated Manchester Central station building on 17 August 2017. The station was opened by the CLC on 1 January 1880 and closed by BR on 5 May 1969. It then fell into disrepair and was used as a car park. The GMCC purchased the disused structure in 1978 and transformed it into the GMEX Building, which was opened by HM the Queen on 21 March 1986. It was rebranded as the Manchester Central Convention Complex in 2007. The clock is thought to be original.

The hub of the Metrolink system is St Peter's Square where a number of lines converge. A four-platform tram station was constructed in 2015–16 in conjunction with the 'Second City Crossing'. Tram No. 3114 is seen alongside the Town Hall Extension building, which was completed in 1934, on 25 March 2017 with a service from East Didsbury to Shaw via Exchange Square. On the right is St Peter's Cross, which is formed out of Portland stone and was erected in 1908.

Tram Nos 3100 and 3068 are seen at Salford Quays on 29 September 2015 with a service from Ashton-under-Lyne to Eccles. This section of line was also used by trams to Media City. The line to Eccles was opened on 6 December 1998. The last remnants of Salford Docks were closed to merchant shipping in 1982 but the area has been substantially redeveloped over the following decades.

The airport line was opened on 3 November 2014. It branched off the East Didsbury line at St Werburgh's Road and continued via Wythenshawe Park, Baguley and Wythenshawe to the airport. It included three sections of ordinary street running; the service line commenced at Victoria. Tram No. 3080 is seen in Hardy Lane at Chorlton on 18 November 2014 heading for the airport.

Numbers 3060 and 3025 are seen at Oldham Mumps with a service from East Didsbury to Rochdale on 8 March 2014. Over the years Oldham was served by five railway stations at Central, Clegg Street, Glodwick Road, Mumps and Werneth but the Metrolink effectively severed the town from the last vestiges of the railway network. Mumps railway station was three short blocks away but the formation is now part of Oldham Way (A62).

The line to East Didsbury was built entirely on a former railway line formation. The original line had been opened by the CLC/MR on 1 January 1880 and was the principal route out of Manchester Central, which passed through Cheadle Heath, Hazel Grove and New Mills. It was closed by BR on 2 January 1967. After lying dormant for over forty-five years it was reopened as a Metrolink line as far as Didsbury on 23 May 2013. M5000 Tram No. 3002 is seen at East Didsbury on 24 May 2013 and will form a service to Rochdale railway station (the then limit of the line).

What was known as 'The Second City Crossing', which provided an alternative route between Victoria and St Peter's Square via Cross Street and Princess Street, was opened on 26 February 2017. Trams Nos 3107 and 3102, both of which were new in 2015, were photographed alongside the National Football Museum in Corporation Street on 23 March 2019 bound for Oldham and East Didsbury respectively.

The Heaton Park Tramway was opened at Easter 1980 and over the years has been extended three times, attaining a running length of just in excess of half a mile. The original section was part of the MCT network, which closed on 10 January 1949. Number 765 was built at the Hyde Road Works and is an original Manchester tram which operated between 1914 and *c.* 1931. It was then used as a works car. After restoration at Crich it returned to Manchester and is seen alongside the tram station/depot on 7 September 1980. The 'California' Car was still operational in 2025.